Mom, Listen!

Mikel Billstrom

The Invitation

Mom,

I need to be honest, I think about death a lot. I am not sure why, but I remember watching my dad being slowly lowered into the ground and I can't help but think he had more to say. I doubt he knew he would die before his mom, and I am so afraid that you would have questions if I were to die today. I know for sure dad would want to make things right with his mom, as well as you and me. I can't imagine not making things right with you before I die. Death is always lurking around the corner. This thought of death drives me crazy because I need you to know what I feel. I need you to know how I have handled our crazy life. I tried to disown you many times because I felt as though you chose a lifestyle over me, but I now know the truth.

I am so scared to write this, but I'm afraid to die with it still inside me. I am so afraid to mess this up or that I'm going to let you down and embarrass you. I am scared to have people judge you. I am afraid the words won't come out right or what I mean to say will be taken wrong. I don't know how I am going to do this, but I do know one thing for sure. I am afraid. I need help writing this, but I have nobody to turn to, much like my childhood. Alone with my thoughts and wondering what it would be like to have someone to turn to.

I need to warn you-you will cry. I know this because I start to cry, just thinking of what I am about to say to you. I know you picture a muscular 35 year-old man, who isn't afraid of anyone or anything, but I am still that little boy who was scared to be alone. I'm still that little boy who was told: "you're the man of the house now!". I am that little boy who wanted to protect you, but was too small to do anything about it. I want that little boy to heal.

Death is always chasing me. I'm afraid of death, and the only way to fearlessly face death is to heal that little boy. I am talking about the boy who wants so badly to be a man, but at the same time doesn't know what that means. I know there is a man inside of me somewhere, but he won't show himself until the little boy is healed. He won't reveal himself unless I tell the truth.

Mom, I need to heal. Will you help me? I need you to listen. HERE IS WHAT I WOULD SAY IF YOU WILL LISTEN. If you're ready, I am prepared to reveal the man that's screaming to come out. The man of my potential.

I am nervous, but I am going to write anyway. I challenge you to embrace all the feelings that surface. I have learned that feelings are not to be avoided. After all, they are called FEELINGS. They are to be felt and used. Will you promise to feel with me? I promise to be quick and not use too many big words:)

The One About Dad's Murder

Mommy,

Where is heaven? I don't know where it is, and you said that's where daddy went, can we visit him? You told me heaven is a better place and that daddy would be happier there. The problem is, I don't know where heaven is and my heart still hurts. My heart hurts mommy. I don't know how to make it stop. When grandma came to the door yesterday and told you about daddy, her heart was hurting too. I want to go to heaven and see daddy, but you said we can't go, yet. When can we go to heaven, mom? I promise to be good! I saw dad on the news last night. Who put him in the river? Why did he have a white blanket on? Was he cold? I hope I can see him on Saturday when he gets back from heaven. If heaven is good, why is everyone crying about him being there? What's happening mom? Why is everyone crying? Why does my heart feel broken? When will I see Daddy again?

• • •

I remember you walking down the alley and halfway you collapsed to your knees. You had me go to the park with Phil and Dan. My dad had been missing for several days so when grandma opened the door with tears in her eyes, I knew why. You were trying to protect me, but it didn't work. A child can't be protected from a loss like that. It changes everything forever. I didn't know what was going on back then, and I didn't think I would never see my dad again. You had me watch the news that night and I remember it so vividly. I remember watching the stretcher carried up the rocky river bank. I don't know why you had me watch the news then, but I do now. It's a memory I hold close. While it's not the perfect memory, it's a memory of my dad. I don't have many of them and all of them are worth keeping.

A 6-year-olds mind doesn't understand death fully, but the heart feels… It never forgets. My journey has often been lonely with many unanswered questions. I didn't fully understand what you meant when you talked about his death, and yet I knew that my life would be forever changed. I still to this day wonder if people know the pain. The pain of not being able to sit with your dad, to hear funny stories from his childhood or talk about the weather. I haven't had any of those experiences and never will because another man took that from me. It's not fair and I sometimes wonder if anyone can fill that void. But I know better, I know that void can't be filled. I feel like nobody understands the pain of these unanswered questions.

The One When I'm The Man of The House

Dan is my Dad now and I am glad you found him. He said, "It's a commitment, not a hobby!" I don't want to go back, but I'm the man of the house now. Dad said so. It's my job to protect you and Phil because he won't be there. Why won't he come with? I don't understand! If he wants to be our dad, why does he just let us leave? Maybe if I do a good job protecting you and Phil- he'll want to be with us again. I am going to do my best and make him want to be with us again, promise and cross my heart! What does being a man mean? I am 9 and people call me a young man! I don't know what it means, but I'm the man of the house now!

. . .

When we moved back to Arizona this time, it was not good. I still to this day don't know why you decided to go back when the first time was a disaster. This second time changed me. The bad outweighed the good. However, the experience continues to shape my adult life. I am glad it all happened, but it wasn't easy-especially for you.

After my dad's death, it was nice to have another man in my life and a man willing to be my stepdad. I now call that man dad, but after a few years you guys decided to go your separate ways. I need to thank you for bringing him into my life. His presence made me feel chosen, but when he left, I felt like it was my fault. I didn't know you both were fighting demons every step of the way.

The words we hear as kids affect us forever. I never knew they would affect me so much and I didn't realize how much until I was almost 30. I wanted to protect you from the dangers of the world but I couldn't protect you from you. I failed. I was told "you're the man of the house" right before we left Minnesota. The worst part of our lives happened in Phoenix. When we went back, it got worse. Way Worse! But I wouldn't change a thing because, within this hardship, my life was saved. I know these next few letters might be hard for you, but we must revisit these tough times, no matter how bad it hurts mom. It's part of healing the boy, and I need your help.

The One When Kids Know More Than We Think

Mom,

Why don't we have a home? Is it because you give all your money to that guy to smoke more of that stuff? When you make me get out of the van and play basketball at the park, sometimes I pretend to leave you and I watch you smoke it because I know it makes you happy. I like seeing you happy. But afterwards, you become really mean and this scares me because I know I will be in trouble. I hope we can have a home again someday. It gets so hot outside and I can't sleep good because I want to keep you safe. I'm always watching out for the guys, to make sure they don't hurt you again. I like it when people let us sleep on their couch and give us ice cream, but we always leave again. The teachers keep asking where I live and I say "I don't know" and then they ask a lot of questions. But don't worry mom, I don't tell them the truth, just like you told me because I don't want them to take me away from you and Phil. I know better and hope you're proud of me. I want you to be proud of me, mom. I am supposed to be the man of the house, but we don't have one…

• • •

I didn't know how bad it was about to get, Mom. I didn't know your personal struggles and I didn't know exactly what it was that you were doing, but I did know our family struggles were related. We would get into some tricky situations and as a little kid I couldn't connect the dots, but looking back it all makes sense. Kids know more than we give them credit for. We would run out of money and you would send Phil and I to ask strangers for money, and it worked out for a while. But then it didn't work because I knew better and was too ashamed to ask.

I knew things were really bad when you would ask Phil and I to steal people's purses.I couldn't do it. I would make some excuse and hope that you didn't get upset. I knew it was wrong and I also knew you didn't want us to do it, but drugs make people do funny things. Maybe it wasn't even the drugs, maybe it was you trying to provide for us after spending all our money; Either way, they're related.

You're stronger than you know, mom, and I hope someday you know your own strength. I wish I could have helped you more back then, but I was only 10 or 11. I really wish I could've helped because it was about to get way worse.

The One About Him

Mom,

Why does he hit you, mom? I tried to stop him from hitting you, but he gets really mad when he doesn't get money. Why won't you let me call 911?! Why doesn't he help unload the semi-trucks? He's bigger and stronger than you. I don't like him and don't want him around anymore. I wish I could stop him, but he's a grown-up, and I'm not strong enough. Every time he leaves, I feel better, but he always comes back. Why do you like him, mom? I wish you didn't even know him. Nobody will ever hurt you when I'm big with muscles. I'm sorry.

• • •

When we saw him walking down the street, and you called his name, "Detroit! Detroit!" I knew life was about to get really, really bad again. I'm so sorry you went through this Mom. I didn't know what "helping the truckers" meant. Now I do…he was using you to make money. He made you feel significant like you were wanted, and when you'd come back with cash, he would show you even more "love." Who uses a city as a name, anyway? I know it was just his street name, but fuck him. I get so angry thinking about this! A man who preys on vulnerable women is a piece of shit in my book. He had the ability to know when a woman felt alone and helpless like most predators do. You've never felt good enough, and he knew that. In some sick way, he knew how to make you feel important and valued. I understand now, and I am so sorry. I cannot imagine the shame, guilt, and sadness you must live with. You did what you thought was right at the time. I don't judge you.

These realizations have affected me forever. I'm sure they still affect you to this day. I felt like a failure-so helpless. I was too young and small to help, and once I became big enough to protect people, I did. Any time a guy was an asshole to a woman in front of me, I wanted to kick his ass, and most of the time I did. I wish I could meet Detroit as an adult now, but then again, I don't want to go back to jail..

Throughout my childhood, I've always had an enormous desire to save people, but I kept failing. I often wondered why that feeling was *soo* strong. That feeling still follows me today, but time has a way of changing things.

The One In The Laundromat

Mom,

I don't like hanging out in the laundromat all day. I know it's hot outside, but this place is so boring. I am happy we aren't around Detroit anymore, he's mean. I don't like him. Why are the two men outside fighting- is it because they're drunk and stupid? I wish we had a place to go. I'll buy you a house someday, mom, and we will never have to worry about not having a place to go -ever again. I promise. Just wait and see, mom.

• • •

I hated that street in Phoenix "Van Buren" because anytime I looked up and saw that sign, it made me realize more hard times were coming. Broadway and many parts of south Phoenix all come to mind when I think back to these most challenging periods of our lives. I remember sitting wherever we could to stay out of the sun and danger. Mom, when you're clean and sober, you are one of the most loving and caring people I have ever known. But during this chapter of our lives, that wasn't the case. I know these hard times still haunt you to this day. I knew why we were homeless, and I started to become hopeful that one day things would be different.

After learning about my dad jumping into a river to save a man, I have always wanted to be a hero of some sort, and I thought a house would save you. It's weird to see how the past repeats itself. To be honest mom, I still feel like a failure for not buying you that house yet. I still worry about you to this day being homeless in Minnesota. Buying you your very own home was a childhood promise, and I'm not sure it will ever be fulfilled. I'm not sure that it *can* be fulfilled. Should I carry that burden around? No, of course not! But I do... I'm sorry, mom.

The One About The Homeless Man

Mom,

Where are you? I don't know what to tell my little brother Phil. I know you'll come back, you always come back, but this man you left us with is weird. He gives my tummy that funny feeling you taught me to listen to. I woke up to him standing at the edge of my bed just looking at me. Phil and I went to play at the park and never came back because I had a bad feeling. Not having a home, I've learned to trust my tummy, and I had to get out of that man's house. The last time I heard from you, the guy you left us with told us you tried to call. He said he heard someone hit you and say: "Get off the phone bitch." If you're not coming back, I have to get us out of here. The day goes fast when you play at the park all day, but at the end of the day, parents started asking questions. They wanted to know where my mom was, so I just made up an excuse and we pretended to walk away, but we had nowhere to go, so we slept in the slide, the tube slide.

It's weird being on the streets all day, I mean normally we had no home, but at least I had you here to help me. I think we will be OK because I've watched you survive like this so many times. I'm just 10 though, and I'm scared, mom. I heard really loud people in the middle of the night talking about hurting people, but I just kept quiet because I knew it was trouble. Parks at night are scary, just like you say. Phil asked me where you were, and I didn't know what to tell him. I somehow told him, "we'll be ok! I know mom is coming back. You always come back, but it's been a couple of weeks now, and I'm starting to get worried. If you do come back, we won't be there, and you'll think we died and went to heaven.

• • •

The next day we were wandering around the neighborhood, and we found this old homeless man in a small wooded area. He was kind to us and let us sit around his little fire. It was right behind the grocery store. In the grocery stores' dumpster they threw away perfectly good food because it expired that day, so Phil and I would gather a bunch of it and bring it to him. He really appreciated that, and it felt good to know we helped him.. I loved the feeling of bringing him food and cooking over the fire together. I felt important, but the next day the garbage can was sealed, and we couldn't get in, I came back to the camp and I told him, "I can't do it." He said "What? can't do what?" I told him, "I can't do it! I can't get the food!". Then he got quiet. After what seemed like forever, he told me, "Don't you ever say that!" I didn't know what he was talking about, and I asked him, "Don't say what?". He said, "Don't you ever say that you can't do it, you can do anything you want to as long as you keep getting better, and *you* don't give up." I sat there in silence because he seemed so angry and then he asked: "Do you know why I am homeless?". I softly murmured, "Because you don't have a home?"

That's when he told me that he used to own businesses, but he chose drugs over his business and his wife. The homeless man told me he'll get it all back as soon as he's done feeling sorry for himself. I don't know what any of it meant but I knew he was angry and I didn't feel safe around him, so we left. We didn't know where to go. We started walking toward the creepy man's house again, just to see if you were there. As we were getting ready to walk up the street, I saw you standing there. You looked horrible. You had a black eye and you immediately started crying and said you were sorry. I did not know what you meant, I was just happy to see you. Within the next couple of days, you called Aunty Bev and asked her to come get us from Minnesota, and she came down immediately.

That 60-second conversation with a homeless man changed my life forever. It took 14 years, but it did! In fact, it might have been the most important moment in my life. I didn't understand why at the time, but I would soon enough.

The One About Hard Decisions

Mom,

I miss you. Every night when I go to bed, I hug this little stuffed animal and pretend you're hugging me goodnight. I wish you would call. I know you're not doing great with those guys. I sure love having a bed to sleep in, and I think you would like it here, too.

Aunty Bev made the trip home fun. We stopped at "The Badlands" and Mount Rushmore. Aunty said these stops would help us have fun because we've had enough bad times already. I miss you, and I don't know if you're ok. I am not sure if I'll ever see you again but it's sometimes easy to distract myself when I'm playing with my cousins. Sometimes I don't worry about you all day. When I go to bed, though, I cry all over again. I asked Phil if he misses you and he just says he doesn't think you're coming back. Will I ever see you again? I hope so, but I am pretty sure I won't, and it makes me cry inside. I cry inside because I don't want Phil to worry any more than he needs to. I miss you and pray for you to come back every night. Please come back, mom! I promise to do better this time. Mom, please come back, please!

• • •

You made sure we had one good meal before we left- Arby's! You wanted to make us feel loved before went our separate ways. I did feel loved and cared for , and it was a nice change. Something unexpected happened. Sometimes moments turn into long-term coping strategies. I made the connection that fast-food means feeling loved and cared for…which caused me problems as an adult. Anytime I felt stressed or overwhelmed I would overeat junk food in search of that feeling. In every McDonalds or Taco Bell meal I searched for the answer that everything was going to be alright, and most importantly, that I'm loved. These connections are the easiest to overlook because they're often hidden in the details of everyday life. Can you think of similar moments? I bet you might connect love to the wrong things if you reflect hard enough. Look carefully, and you'll discover them, I promise.

I still to this day go to sleep worrying about you. In some ways, things are the same. I have always prepared myself for your funeral. I have prepared myself for the moment I get the news. As a kid, you would continuously tell me, "You will be happy when I'm gone." I can tell you that nothing is farther from the truth. . You tell yourself that because you are mad at yourself, and you project that anger at me. . It's not true. Stop.

Thank you though for being brave enough to make hard decisions. I know it wasn't easy to admit you weren't able to keep us safe and cared for in Arizona. I love you for that strength, and I wish you would see this strength more often, but you have a foggy mirror. We'll talk about that later. In these moments, admitting we have problems is the first step to overcoming them. Admitting your faults does not make you weak, it makes you brave. And it kept us safe back then. It was the right decision, mom.

Aunt Bev took us in and provided a safe place for us. She didn't need to, but she loved you and was there for you when you needed it most. It's easy to take peoples' help for granted sometimes, but she sacrificed a lot for us. I'll forever be thankful for that, and the countless other people who took us in for a night or two during our most challenging moments. I'll never forget their generosity, and it's influenced me to be there for people in my life. Not enabling but helping: I've learned there is a difference.

You did make it home six months later. We cannot run from ourselves and if we avoid our problems, we can be sure they are on our tail. Our issues travel well. They're always there.

The One With The Broom

Mom,

I tried! Why can't you see that I tried!!!!??? All the dust wouldn't go into the dustpan with one swipe!! I'm so sick of not being good enough. You hit me over and over with the boomstick, and for the first time, I cried from a beating. I didn't cry from the broom hitting me, I've been hit with way worse. I cried because every time you hit me with it, you said "Can't you do anything right?!", "Are you stupid?!". I could never make you happy and you blamed me for everything in your life!! That's why I ran out of the house!

Fuck you, mom! I'm not your son anymore!

• • •

This moment happened when I was 13. The memory came back to haunt me during college football at 20 years old. I had just intercepted a pass and ran for a touchdown during practice, but there was anger brewing in me. I wasn't reaching my potent because my knees were acting up. I wasn't as fast as usual. When I caught the ball, I made a perfect read; I knew exactly where to be, where the wide receivers were going to be, and I jumped the ball, taking it all the way for a touchdown.

I felt like I finally broke through that season and made the play despite my knees. I went back to the huddle, and my coach said: "Billstrom! Attack the ball at it's highest point!". I didn't get a compliment nor the acknowledgment that I scored a touchdown. Instead, I heard "Can't you do anything right?!" and I lost it. I took my helmet and shoulder pads off, threw them at the coach and said, "If your old ass can do it better, here you go!!" I walked off the field and quit.

Football saved my life growing up, so why would I throw in the towel ? I quit because I didn't feel good enough, even when trying my hardest. It never was good enough. Just like that day, I tried to collect dust into a dustpan. It wasn't what the coach said; it's what I heard. I quit because of the words I've heard before...I quit because of what I was told as a kid.

When you hit me with that broomstick, it wasn't me you were mad at, you were upset with yourself. You were still battling that little voice in your head, that makes you feel worthless like you can't do anything right. You were repeating your history all over again.

Unfortunately, we remember pain more than we remember the love. Our past comes back to haunt us if we do not take the time to understand it or at least give it meaning. If we run from our past, it becomes the director of our lives. We keep those same fears on repeat, and we end up running like sheep being herded in any direction the herder, or fear, decides.

At some point, I was sick of running and found out it if I turn around and face the past, I have a fighting chance to live my own life, and have a future. A future not as a prisoner of the past.t. I couldn't let the past repeat itself so I made the decision to walk back on that football field. The good times in life take care of themselves but pain repeats itself if allowed to do so.

Your mom tied you to a couch and beat you with a horsewhip all day. I can't imagine the things she told you growing up, and it makes me so sad seeing you not believe in yourself. I'm sorry you had to go through that. I'm sorry that pain and suffering manifests itself in ugly ways as an adult. I'm sorry you still fight those words every day of your life, even if they're not true. Your past might be trying to relive itself.

Some things are starting to make sense to me; hurt people hurt people…

The One About Moving Out

Mom,

I am not moving again!!!! I just started football, and I've moved in the middle of the season two years in a row. I'm done! I'm 15, almost 16, and I can take care of myself. You better sign the papers when I ask, or I'll just run away. I just made friends and I finally seem to fit in somewhere. I am not moving!! Football is the only chance I have to make it…It's the one thing I am good at, and I won't let you take it from me.

• • •

We moved almost 20 times before I made this decision. Thank you for knowing that it would be best for me. I know you weren't happy, but it worked out. I worked two part-time jobs and rented a room for a little bit. It was hard working, going to school, and playing football.

Six months later, I was blessed by a family who let me live with them until I graduated. I will forever be grateful for Kevin and his amazing parents Bev and Steve. Grace has shown up in my life when I least expected it.

The room I was renting wasn't a great situation, but I didn't have many options at the time. It worked out for the best, and I am not sure how life would have turned out if it wasn't for that decision to move. . You seem to know what is best for me, even if it's not living with you. Just like calling Aunt Bev to pick us up from Arizona, you made another good decision. Thank you.

We are more alike than I like to admit.

The One About Awards

Mom,

Where were you last night? I was the only one there without parents, I made 1st team All-Conference, defensive back of the year and 1st team all-area. You were always proud of me but you never drove up for a single game. Dan never even wanted me to play football and would say "You're a dreamer, be more realistic!". I wish you were there last night. I had a really good season, and all my hard work paid off. I wish you would have seen some of my games. I was undersized, but I played pissed off. I know you came to a couple of games when I was a sophomore, but it's not the same as a varsity football game.

• • •

Something weird happened with football. I worked my ass off, and I finally saw it pay off. I saw that effort does make a difference, as opposed to growing up helpless. This was the first time I set goals in my life, followed up by hard work. The ingredients of success, setting goals and hard work, actually works. .

Football saved my life in many ways. The first way football shaped me, is that it gave me a group of friends who didn't care where I came from or what kind of clothes I wore. They only cared about me helping them win. Secondly, football provided an outlet. I was angry and took it out on everyone who crossed my path. Football kept me focused and let me use anger in a legal way.

One reason people remain in the same spot forever , is because they do not feel they can influence the outcome. That thought process traps people exactly where they are; it leads to resentment and blame. Blame makes us feel like it's ok to quit. It makes us feel that our life isn't our responsibility- it's a learned helplessness, and it is a trap we can find ourselves in if we aren't careful.

I set a goal to play college football in 5th grade, and everyone laughed at me because of my size. I carried that chip on my shoulder until I was in college. I only played for a small division 3 college, but I made it. It flew by, and the next thing I know I am playing my last college game. I still have a hard time describing all that I felt that day. Every game in the past four years,

I would look into the stands hoping someone was there to watch me! But nobody was ever there. I was warming up as usual, but something felt different this time. I took my helmet off, expecting to see no one, glanced up, and for the first time, I had someone glancing back at me. It was a weird feeling; I experienced sadness, rage, and hope. I prayed that I played good enough to hear those words. The words I've been craving my whole life. "I'm proud of you Mikel! I knew you could do it!". The words that rarely hit my ears until that day.

It meant a lot to me, and I'm glad you got to see me before that season of my life vanished . There were many 5 am gym sessions that nobody knew about and sprints until I puked. The one thing that bothers me is that people in our family think hitting goals is all about natural talent..That's not even close to the truth, and when people tell themselves that, it gives them a reason to avoid their potential. Don't avoid your potential, mom.

The One About Being Scared

Mom,

I think she is pregnant, and I am not ready to be a dad. I don't know what to do. I guess I don't have a choice, but I need to be there for my baby. I will do my best. I need to graduate to have a shot in this world and find a way to break the cycle. I am scared mom. I don't want to mess this up. This is too important.

...

We denied it for months, but we knew she was pregnant. I was a horrible boyfriend. I continuously needed attention from girls and wasn't there for her when she needed me the most. Hardship had become my default, or normal existence, and when she was going through a hardship I brushed it off. I neglected to see her hardship as serious. If I'm honest, I was extremely selfish and was too busy to notice how much I was screwing up.

I never knew how difficult being a parent was and I wish I would have done things differently. I know you did not always feel like the best parent, but I messed it up worse- way worse! I can never take actions or words back, but I can keep trying to make it right. I am unsure if my daughter will ever want to have a relationship with me, but I will not give up.

I did end up graduating HS with a 1.8 GPA, and even that was a miracle. I thought there was no way I would graduate , but I had a lot of help from people who pushed me. Kevin's mom, Bev, and all my football coaches motivated me to stay on track.

You did show up for my graduation. I was surprised, but you made it. I cried.

The One About Failing Again

Mom,

I can't believe this happened, but I guess it's expected in our family. I wish I had some money or that I could receive a loan from someone for a lawyer. , But here I am. Again, I have no back up in life. The guy I hit had more than enough money, knew all the right people in town, and I was the poor new kid. I had no chance without a lawyer.

I am letting Makenzie down and it breaks my heart to know she's going to wonder where I went. I am sure her mom is letting her know exactly what kind of piece of shit I am. I don't know what to do. I'm here for 120 days and then there are 2 months of house arrest once I get out. Oh, and let's not forget about $15,000 in restitution I have to somehow pay on a dishwashers pay. That shouldn't take long!

I hope you'll come visit me but I'll be fine alone. I have no idea what life will bring after this, but I'm sure I'll find out soon enough

. . .

I felt so out of place, and alone, very alone. I never imagined my temper and a childhood promise to you would land me in jail. I wasn't sure what life would bring after this. I ruined any contact I had with my daughter, was now a felon, and somehow ended up in a cell with a person who murdered a family with a hammer. He was a pretty big pussy and I was hoping I would have a chance to break his face…

At first, I felt sorry for myself and then I started to feel something build up inside me that I haven't felt for awhile. I felt like I couldn't fight my way out of the problem. I had to suffer the consequences of my actions- and suffer I did.

After I got out, I learned very fast that getting a place to live or a job as a felon wasn't easy. It was almost impossible! I couldn't see myself doing anything good with my life. I pictured myself barely surviving and scheming like everyone in my family. I was fighting a battle with myself. Constantly wondering if I would ever get it together? It wasn't looking good because if I wasn't fighting, I was looking for my next fight. I didn't learn the lesson I was meant to learn or maybe I was too addicted to the adrenaline, or the instant validation of "winning".

Blaming people was easier than dealing with my problems, but the outcome of that behavior was believing I was a helpless victim and I'm not. So instead, I started to beat myself up. I punished myself mentally, emotionally and physically. I was sick of myself. There was an ongoing battle inside me, I either could choose to fight all the idiots around me and add more time to my sentence, or keep my cool and get out of jail on time. Luckily all confrontations just ended with people talking shit and I was oddly disappointed. Violence was weirdly satisfying and I craved a battle. Winning a fight made me feel significant. It made me feel good enough. When my opponent hits the ground unconscious, I would feel like I finally did something right.

Oh, and thanks for visiting me. Once.

The One About The Rich Girl

Mom,

I have been hanging out with this rich girl. I feel myself becoming resentful sometimes; her dad owns a company and he pays for her car and everything. Anytime she needs help, her family is always there. Her name is Katie, and she's just wonderful- she is kind, pretty, and I might date her. But she also seems like "one of the boys" so who knows. She's a friend and that is probably the best place for her in my life.

She keeps pushing me to do something bigger with my life- something other than washing dishes or warehouse work. This is probably because she sees me barely able to pay $350 for a room to rent. I mean my checks are only $250 every two weeks after child support and taxes. I don't think she understands how limited my employment options are with a felony. She says I should try selling cars. She saw an ad in the paper and it said "no experience necessary," but I don't think I could do anything like sales. I can barely look at people in their eyes without feeling *like people are judging me. She even offered to buy me new dress pants, shirts, and a couple of ties. I don't know. I don't think it's a good idea and not my thing, but she says I should at least show up for an interview. I think it's a waste of time, though. I am not good enough for a job like that.*

• • •

Sometimes we need other people to believe in us more than we believe in ourselves. Katie was that person then, and my wife is that person now.

How many times can these tragedies and triumphs happen? Where do these forks in the road come from? I didn't think I could excel at sales and I was right because I was awful. Have you ever seen a person with low self-esteem thrive at sales when they are repeatedly told "leave me alone" or "not interested" over and over? No, and I was about to be fired, but first I had to sabotage myself before actually failing at something. Of course it is easier to self-sabotage than fail. I could easily find another obstacle to put in my way just so I would not have to hear the words "You are not good enough". Self sabotaging was my way out. .

I took a chance at sales,I wasn't succeeding, and old patterns started to appear . I missed a probation meeting I wasn't aware of, and now I had to go back to jail for 12 days. I just started this job. Why do the cards of life end up this way?? I know how it happens. I'm a fuck-up, as usual, and they for sure are going to fire me now.

The last thing I wanted to do was tell my new boss that I had to go to jail, but there was no way around it. I had to have the talk and just hope for the best. The next day I went to talk to my manager, Barry. I nervously approached his office. I could feel myself instantly start to sweat, and my face was bright red. There was a bright side, though. I thought instead of continuing to suck and meeting my fate of eventually getting fired, I could just be let go. It wouldn't be my fault because I was in jail. Phew! I had a way out!

But then when I was telling him about my upcoming jail time, he replied with something totally unexpected. He said, "How many days?". I told him "12 days". He paused, rubbed his head, and replied, "See you in a couple of weeks!". My mouth was so dry that I could barely speak but I was able to muster up a "huh?" And he just repeated himself, "See you in a couple of weeks!". After I gathered myself and realized

I wasn't getting fired, I felt a massive surge of energy. At the time, I still didn't believe I could succeed in this position, but I had a second chance, and my life had a chance to finally change.

The One Saying Goodbye

Mom,

If you're reading this, I'm sure you know it's too late. I am already gone. I am sorry, I can't do this anymore! I can't seem to do anything right, and I am so sick of struggling with the same things over and over! I just wanted you to know that I love you and it's not your fault. I keep messing up, and this place would be better off without people like me. I was hoping to fight my way up in this game called life, but when the cards you were dealt are worthless, why play the game? Why play when the odds are so stacked against you? I know you're going to blame yourself but don't, it's my fault. I chose to keep screwing up. I can't figure out why, so I am just going to end it. I hope you, Phil, Tjay, Anna, and Dan come to my funeral. I have always been fearful that nobody would show up at my funeral. Please tell my daughter that I tried and that I wanted to be in her life. I've tried so many times, and obviously, nothing is going to work out for me... I'm done! My life is pointless! I'll leave this on my bed, so my roommate finds it. Goodbye. I love you.

• • •

The pain of life is too much sometimes, and this was one of those times. The odds were stacked against me from the start, and I was not going to fight an uphill battle for my entire life. I kept making the same mistakes, and when I finally did seem to be on the right track, things would still go wrong. I didn't know what to do. By some miracle, I was able to keep my job after going to jail, but I was failing terribly. I was truly horrible at sales and didn't think I could ever be successful . I always thought to myself, "I should have known better!". I caught wind that they were going to fire me because I didn't even come close to hitting my quota again. The one chance I had at a decent life was slipping away. So I gave up…

• • •

I was standing there watching the train get closer and closer, the whistle blowing so loudly that I could feel it in my soul. The conductors obviously saw me standing there, and they were trying their best to stop me. I ignored it.

Here it comes, it's only 50 feet away! The loud rumble is so loud that I can't hear anything and everything seems to be in slow motion. It's getting closer 30ft, 25ft, 20ft… I'm doing it-I don't have to suffer or fight anymore.. 10ft, 5ft!

 And then, out of nowhere, I was pushed off the tracks! But by who? I still have no idea. I think about that moment and maybe an angel stepped in and pushed me off, or was it me? Did I step off knowing I had more fight left in me? To this very day, I am not sure if I stepped off or some spiritual force pushed me off. I guess It was not my time. A shift started to happen after that moment. I didn't know what it was, but I felt something I couldn't put my finger on. Something started to bubble up in me.

The next day I was going to quit my job. They couldn't fire me if I quit and I thought that it would look better if I decided to get another job. But I didn't end up quitting my job. I planned on it but I chickened out and left work like it was just another day.

On the way home, something strange happened, and my life would never be the same.

The One About The Student

Mom,

I bought my first book today. I don't know why I had the urge to buy a book, but something happened on my way home from work. I spent my own money on a book about how to be a successful salesman. I only have 26 bucks, and I just spent 17. I had a very shitty day yesterday, and I almost made a terrible mistake, but things I can't explain have been happening lately. I don't want to sound crazy, so maybe one day I'll tell you more in person. Just wish me luck. I'm feeling pretty positive and hopeful right now. I don't know where you are or what you're getting into lately, but just know I'm ok. Well, I think anyway, I guess we'll see. I want to be ok for once. Ok is better than wanting to die.

. . .

Those haunting words crept back…

"Don't ever say that!" I thought I must be losing my mind…"Why do you think I'm homeless?!?! Don't you ever say that!! I'll get it all back once I'm done feeling sorry for myself!". On my way home a random voice in my head started telling me not to think or say certain things. I was freaked out, and I felt goosebumps all up and down my arms because I realized something. I recognized that voice. He was back- it was the homeless man who yelled at me about getting food out of the dumpster! I've heard of flashbacks before. I must have been under a lot of stress because I have not thought of him in over 14 years. In fact,he never crossed my mind again after that day he yelled at me. Did a ghost of my past visit me? Is this my version of *The Christmas Carol?*

Right after I heard his voice, on my way home, I bought my first book. I called in sick the next day and read the whole book. This was extremely out of character for me because I've never bought or read a book in my life. I know you think I was a great student, but I barely graduated high school, and I cheated my way through the entire thing. I was not the kind of guy who read books, and especially not the guy who buys books.

In that book, for the first time, I had someone encouraging me, telling me I could do it and that I can never give up. My life has never been the same since that moment, and now I'm obsessed with books. I kept reading and setting goals, and something unexpected happened. I became an excellent salesman and eventually, one of the best. Books literally saved my life and I have been a reader ever since.

I don't know who that homeless man was, and I sometimes feel like it was all in my imagination, but he was there, and the student was ready. Of course, I've had people tell me I'm "good enough" and "don't give up," but I wasn't prepared to listen to them. This man was put into my life for a reason, and his timing was divine. If the student isn't ready, the teacher is hopeless because all the words fall on deaf ears.

The road ahead would not become any easier, but I was committed to the act of continuously striving to become the best version of myself. Maybe even turn my life around, and finally make something of myself. The student was ready. The question remained: would books be enough?

The One About Dealers

Mom,

I will never do that again. I am done!! I will not answer your calls or have you in my life. This is the last time I ever pay a man you owe money for something you shouldn't be doing in the first place. Why do drug dealers think it's a good idea to loan people money while helping them ruin their lives?

It's all so f'n stupid! I can't take it anymore, and every time I do this I feel the urge to beat the shit out of them, but I have been down that road before. It never ends well. Those cowards think they intimidate people, and I wish one would say something smart to me...

Mom, Please don't call me, don't show up at my job or anywhere else. I am too focused on getting my shit together to deal with your stupid choices. This has been going on my whole life, and I finally have a chance to be someone, and I don't need you pulling me down. I just can't. You will not be in my life until you're clean!! Period!!

• • •

I loved the feeling of being there for you and helping you fix your problems. At times it seemed like I was addicted to helping you, but at some point, I gave up. Something clicked, I realized I wasn't going to be part of that life anymore. I had to remove myself. I tried everything I knew: I loved you, hated you, disowned you, and encouraged you; I made excuses for you. I felt helpless, and like nothing I did mattered. I decided to focus on myself and see if I could break the patterns in our family. I had to make it one way or another.

As normal, I can't save you. I didn't know what else to do, and those familiar feelings of being a failure came rushing back. However, this time something was different. It felt like I was underwater trying to find the surface and when I finally did, I took the biggest breath of my life. I am not sure what, but something changed in me.

Deep in my heart, I was hoping you'd pick me over that lifestyle. Why did I need to be chosen so bad? Is love an action more so than words? I knew you loved me because you said so, but I wanted to see that love in action. I wanted to be chosen. I wanted to matter to you- more than any drug this world could offer.

I didn't want to be part of your life anymore, and I ignored every call until I didn't need to ignore you because you stopped trying. I changed my number and made sure you didn't have it. I gave up on you.

The One About The Lady In The Snow

Mom,

I miss you! It's been a couple of years now of keeping my distance, but I wish we could have a good relationship. This disconnect is familiar and seems oddly comfortable, but as I get older, I start to realize how precious relationships are. I quit my job and I am going to start something that matters. I don't know what yet but I will make something happen. I must allow good to come from these bad times. I feel that's why I was put through these hardships, to make the experiences pay! I can choose to use them for good or let them use me. Maybe someday we'll be able to have this talk in person. I miss you and hope you're okay. I don't even have your phone number or know if you have a phone.

. . .

Two days later I was bored and decided to go to a Barnes and Noble. And for some reason, I didn't want to go to any of the ones near my house. I needed a change of pace and decided to head to the downtown Minneapolis Barnes and Noble. I have no idea why I picked that one because I hate driving downtown, and not only that, but I hate paying for city parking even more! I walk in, and there is that familiar excitement of when I go to a new book store. I guess it's me hoping there will be a hidden gem that could change my life-the book I haven't seen before, the book that has all of life's answers in it. But as usual, almost all bookstores have all the same books. I decided to pick up this random book I've seen many times, but never opened it because it had "God" in the title and I wasn't into that. But curiosity got the best of me, and I picked it up because it was catchy. It was called "When God Winks at You." I grabbed it, bought a coffee at Starbucks, and picked a seat right by the window facing the sidewalk of Nicollet Ave. I've always been a people watcher, but there weren't many people out because it was snowing giant snowflakes, and I could barely see anything.

The falling snow was calming as it muffled the city noise. I hesitantly cracked the book open and started to read about how sometimes God gives you unexpected signs. I read a little story about how it hasn't snowed in this particular part of Texas in forever, and someone prayed for snow as a sign they would be healed from their sickness, or something like that. I can't remember exactly, but I wasn't impressed. It snowed, they were healed- blah blah blah. Who cares, random things happen all the time, and it can all be explained. I flipped to the next story, started to read, and at that moment, I noticed someone coming down the sidewalk. Curiosity got the best of me because I haven't seen a soul during the storm. She was walking super fast, bundled up to head to toe, walking quickly with multiple bags in each hand. As she gets closer, she zooms right past my window, literally 2ft in front of my face.

No way! It can't be! I run outside and screamed, "Excuse me, Excuse me," but there is no response; she kept walking. I went back inside, thinking I was going crazy. Maybe I was hoping it was you, who knows. I sat back down, opened my book again, but I couldn't let go of that feeling. I go back outside, jog down the block, and as I catch up she moved out of my path. I think I scared her because she seemed a little startled and said: "Excuse me, honey!". I instantly recognized her voice, but she appeared to be standoffish or embarrassed. I asked her how she was doing, why she's running around in a storm, and we sat there in a snowy awkwardness. She almost treated me like a stranger and had to rush off to catch a bus. I hugged her and told her that I loved her.

That woman was you, mom. My little nonchalant prayer turned into you rushing past me outside a Starbucks window. God winked at me that day. The ball was now in my court. If I wanted a relationship with you, I would have to do my part, and since that day, I have done everything in my power to have a relationship with you.

The One About Being More Alike Than I Knew

Mom,

We had a weird but awesome moment today. We were sitting in Lake Calhoun trying to cool down because it's like 100 degrees outside. I've been making an effort to connect and have moments with you no matter what. Even when you're coming down from bad decisions or whatever else. Something has changed in me, and I want more of these moments connecting with you. I'm sorry I can't let you live with me again. We tried that, and I can't do it again. If you're making poor decisions, I shouldn't make it easier for you and enable you. I'm sorry. But what you said today caught me off guard. I've never heard you speak of it before. You said "Your dad would be proud of you, Mikel" and I asked a little about him and you told me a few stories. Then you said, "I wonder how my dad would feel about me still messing up all the time?". I can't believe I've never asked. This short conversation opened my eyes to something.

• • •

Since this moment I've asked you so many questions, but you've avoided answering them because it's painful. All these years, I've felt alone in my journey trying to figure out what my dad would think or say. What it would feel like for him to grab my shoulder and tell me, "you can do it" or that he was proud of me. I thought I was the only one, but now I'm connecting the dots, and some things are starting to make sense. I'm beginning to understand you. All these years, I've never tried to understand you because I was too busy worrying about myself and how special my pain and struggles are. I've found out they're not special and I'm not the only one who has them.

Another man took your dad's life, and you know the pain of waiting and wondering if he'll ever come back. You never had your questions answered. You never received that reassuring look that everything is going to be alright. You never were able to experience him looking in your eyes at your wedding and calling you beautiful. You never had him grab your hand and tell you not to give up on yourself and to keep going. He never put his hands on your shoulders, made you look at him and told you you're good enough. There is so much that you never had the chance to experience with your dad. I was too selfish to wonder if it affects you as much as it affects me.

I am sorry, Mom. I know what you're going through and went through. It does not seem fair, and it still fills me with rage, sadness, confusion, and wonder. I know how much this affects us. The cards of life were dealt, and we didn't get a pair of aces, but we must play them.

I wonder what life would be like with our dads there to guide us and answer the hard questions of life. I still wonder how my Dad would handle the tricky situations of me not believing in myself, feeling insecure, and always seeking instant validation from women. What would he say? These questions will never have answers. I'll have to figure them out for myself, and you'll have to do the same.

I never asked about grandpa until I was in my 30's. I guess I was too caught up in myself to ask you any questions about your life. I was too busy feeling sorry for myself. If an event like losing my dad as a young kid affects me forever, it must still affect you. I am sorry for hating you sometimes. I am sorry for not understanding you for the first 33 years of my life. I don't understand myself, but I am slowly peeling back the layers. I've read a lot of grandpas letters; he sure loved you with all of his heart. I think I know how he would answer that question you had that day.

He would say the following:

"I am sorry I left you with so many questions. I'm sorry I didn't have more time with you, it's one of my few regrets. I wish I could have been there for you to cry on, to answer your questions, to reassure you, and with just a look tell you not to be so hard on yourself.. I wish I were there to protect you from some of the pain you've experienced. I wish I was there to teach you how to stand back up when you fall. I'm so sorry for missing special moments and leaving so soon. I guess I am a man of my own convictions and had a wild side that I just couldn't keep in line. Diane, do Dad a favor, take these next words to heart:

Please be kind to yourself, be honest with yourself and know that I'm with you. I know you think you "can't" sometimes, but you can. I know you can. I know you wonder if I am watching, I am. And those times you think you feel me-you're right. I know you're battling something. At times you will win the battle, and other times you will lose the battle, but if you never give up, you will win the war. Your battle is personal and has to be fought by you, Diane. I'm watching and cheering you on…

I love you more than words can express.

Hug the little ones for me,

Dad"

The One When Love Hurts

Mom,

It's fall again, and I start to worry about you. I know you're okay in the summer, but these brutal winters aren't to be played with. It makes it so hard for me to create boundaries and not have you on my couch. I'm newly married, have a dog, and only a one-bedroom apartment. Why should I have to worry about my mom? I guess the answer is I don't have a choice because I love you and love hurts sometimes.

The government pisses me off too because somewhere along the line they've told you you're helpless, but if you do work, they cut off your measly $630 a month. Then you will have zero guaranteed income, no car, and I start to understand why you want to avoid life sometimes. I feel so guilty in some ways. That childhood guilt still kicks my ass. I can't protect you and if I do, is it the right thing to do? I would love to use some magic powers and make all your struggles go away, but I don't think that would be the best way to handle it. I've learned a lot about you throughout the years. You're resilient, and I know this *isn't your first winter, but I still lose lots of sleep not knowing where you are. I hope you're ok, mom.*

. . .

Love is a weird thing. It's so powerful and yet so painful. When you love someone, you hurt when they hurt. You hurt when someone you love is missing. You hurt when someone you love does not treat themselves very well. You hurt when someone you love refuses to believe in themselves. You hurt when someone you love doesn't enjoy their life. You hurt when someone you love blames you for their failures. You hurt when someone you love doesn't show love in the way you expect it to be shown. Love is a two-sided coin, and it sometimes lands on pain-time and time again. .

The other half of love is what they write poems about, all the good stuff that we enjoy so much. The feeling you get when you see someone you love accomplish their dreams, believe in themselves, overcome fear and doubt. When you see them use their courage instead of letting doubt stop them in their tracks. The feeling you get when you see someone that's been hurting for so long have a peaceful moment without fear or stress. I've had those moments with you mom, and I cherish them. I wish they would come along more often, but then they lose their value. If it's all good all the time, life gets pretty dull. Although, it would certainly be easier. That "love" feeling is amazing and can't be replaced. It might feel like those feelings are impossible sometimes, but I promise you they're not. Every day we have a chance to face our fears and use our courage. We have an opportunity to finally tell ourselves the truth, even if it's painful, and when we do, it feels like a heavy weight has been lifted.

I see the truth of love now. Love is connected to pain like black is to white, cold is to hot, and night is to day. Love is painful, love is pure bliss, and most importantly, love is worth it.

The One About Foggy Mirrors

Mom,

I quit a really good paying job over a year ago, and I want to do something to help people, but I am not sure what. Now, I have no income, and things are getting hard again. Is this me sabotaging myself, or maybe things were going too good, and I prefer struggle? I sometimes think that I'm more comfortable in the struggle. I see this look now in my wife's eyes. She believes in me, but she's worried. I don't know what to do. I wish all my problems would just go away and I could help people. I not only want to help people, but in some odd way I feel my soul pulling me to help people believe in themselves. I feel like it's my life's calling. I'm pretty stressed out. Life is hard sometimes.

I'll write again later. I am going to take a long shower and avoid life for a little bit.

...

I took that shower, mom, and the entire bathroom was full of steam. I couldn't see anything after staying in the shower for what seemed like forever. As I was wiping the steam off the mirror, I saw myself and was disgusted with what I saw in the mirror. The person who always messes things up is staring me right in the face, and I turned away, not wanting to look at myself. I tried to look away, but I decided to have a staredown with myself instead. During this staring contest, a bunch of feelings started to come over me. At first, I felt anger, then disappointment, confusion, and a wave of intense anger, almost like hatred. All these different emotions were coming through so fast and in giant waves. One snuck in that I didn't expect. All week I could not stop thinking about that unfamiliar feeling. I was stumped, but eventually, I was able to figure out what it was.

Empathy. I started to see that little boy in me who has been trying to grow up and be the man his whole life. I felt his pain as I looked into his eyes. I could see the innocence, and as I was looking at him, I accidentally let a small smile come over my face. I smiled because I realized something. I realized that kid has not given up. He has wanted to throw in the towel many times, but he keeps fighting. He's struggling to reach his potential but hopefully in the end he will come out on top. I love that little boy- his heart is pure, his intentions are good, and he's always wanted to help people however he could.

As I was thinking about that little boy, I saw him looking back at me in the mirror and I wanted to help him. I kept staring into the mirror, into his eyes and then something hit me right in the gut. I could be that little boy's hero. But something would have to shift first.

I've always had this feeling of wanting to save people, and that feeling has been a constant companion of mine. My dad saved someone's life, and I've always looked up to him for that. My dad isn't here to save me, and if he were here, he still wouldn't be able to save me, because my battle is inside me, and nobody can save me-not even my dad.

As I was looking into the mirror, I saw the man responsible for all my problems. I saw the person who would need to overcome the odds and play the hand he was dealt. I saw a person who could save my life. I saw my hero in the mirror and the only person who is with me for every second of my life. Me.

If I am going to save that little boy inside me, I'll have to reveal the man. The man who takes responsibility for every mistake in his life. The man who doesn't avoid honesty, even if it hurts to have that conversation. The man who can be honest with himself and hold himself accountable for all his actions or lack of effort. The man inside of me has to appear if I want to save that little boy.

If you look hard enough and long enough, you'll realize that if that little girl is going to be saved, the woman must show herself. Your hero is in the mirror, mom. I love you.

The One About Two Different Women

Mom,

I tracked you down and took you out for lunch today. I've been trying to see you even when you're homeless. I have had Thanksgiving in shelters with you. I've found you in the park to hangout on Mother's Day. I brought you tea every morning when you were living in a tent, a block from my apartment. I have committed to having you in my life no matter what, and I am getting pretty good at setting boundaries. I have learned to show love without letting you live on my couch or give you money. I struggle because I could solve some of your problems, but I shouldn't, and I know this. I am not your hero, and I'm ok with that.

As we were driving to lunch today, you made me pull over, you ran out into the intersection, and you gave a homeless man a dollar, your last dollar. You've been doing this your whole life, and I thought, "That's why she's homeless, she can't even hang onto her last dollar!" But then I remembered, that's just you.

I've seen two versions of you my whole life. I've seen the woman who taught me that skin color means nothing and to love all the differences in people. The woman who taught me to fight bullies and never back down to the forces of evil. The woman who does anything to help anyone she can, however she can. That is the woman I know. That is the woman I call mom. She's amazing!

The other side of you isn't the real you. It's just a woman who doubts herself, gets overwhelmed and does whatever she can to avoid the pain of the past. The woman who is doing good, but is scared to death she's going to mess it up again. The woman who tells people they'll be happy when she's dead. The woman who uses people, and then gets upset when they stop helping her. The woman who is ungrateful and feels entitled- the woman who expects everyone should drop what they're doing to help her. But this is NOT the real you. This is you when you and drugs get together. It's NOT the woman I love. It's the woman I can't stand to hear speak or spend a minute with when she shows up, but it's not you.

I wish you could see the woman I see when you look into the mirror...

• • •

The past is the past, and some believe history must repeat itself. I don't think so. The past repeats itself only if we continue to live in it, and we live in it without even realizing it. If we do not learn from past mistakes we will keep suffering the same pain over and over. The past isn't the past-the past is here now because it has molded us into our present. It's here in every moment of our lives constantly reminding us of how we failed, how we shouldn't have said that certain thing, how we should have tried harder, and how we are a victim of our own doing or of someone else's doing. But make no mistake, it's here alive and well. It's trying to keep us hostage. It's comfortable here with us; like an old friend we have outgrown but refuse to let go.

The past will repeat itself until the lesson is learned or until we die. The past isn't to be avoided, Mom. It's to be used. Use the past as a painful reminder, like when we touch a hot stove and know we shouldn't do it again. The past is our friend and wants to teach us, but only when the student is ready. If the student isn't ready the past can't teach. Just like the homeless man in the park when I was a kid, I wasn't ready and 14 years later I was ready.

Please don't let the past slip away, mom. Instead make the past pay, and give it meaning by letting it help you in the present and future. The past is not the enemy, it's your friend, mentor, and wise old teacher. Love the past, for it will make our future. We get to decide how much the past will pay for our trouble. Make it pay, mom.

The One About Pain

Mom,

I asked you some hard questions today. I asked you about your childhood, your past, how you felt as a parent. You've opened up about some things, but for the most part, you change the subject. But you did answer one question this time. Finally. I asked, "What would you want to know if you knew you were going to die tomorrow?". "You said, "I would like to know my kids are okay and that I didn't mess things up too bad!" You said that you didn't like to think about the past because it's painful. I can understand that because I've been asking myself hard questions over the past 5 or 6 years and sometimes I don't like the answers. But, I will not stop asking hard questions because I am starting to understand you. I am connecting a lot of dots.

• • •

What can I say about pain? Pain is always there, no matter what. The only constants in this world are pain, gravity, taxes, death, and some other stuff, but I won't go that deep right now. Love is intertwined with pain, and if the best thing this world has to offer comes with pain, how can we expect to live a life void of pain? We can't and shouldn't hope to.

We must be willing to suffer, or else we cannot truly live. Pain is an essential part of life, we must have a daily serving, or we're missing out. There are many forms of pain. Physical pain, mental pain, spiritual pain, the pain of regret, pain from growth, the pain of losing, pain preparing to win, and every other pain you can think of. It's always there and if you feel no pain right now, please enjoy the moment because the next dose of pain is right around the corner.

The worst pain we can suffer, in my experience, is knowing you are not doing what you should. This kind of pain is different because it's with us no matter how long we pretend it's not there. It makes you feel like you are a rabbit being chased by wolves and you know it's only a matter of time until they catch up to you. We can lie to ourselves and pretend the wolves aren't coming, but we know they'll show up eventually. We will lose the people we love, we will cry when they hurt, we will have our hearts broken, we will feel like a failure, and people will hurt us. We know pain is coming. When we know the enemy is on the way, we can prepare for battle- and this makes all the difference.

We must stand up tall and face the many packages pain comes in. After all, it's unavoidable, so we might as well take it on voluntarily. When we show the courage to face pain, it takes the edge off; it doesn't scare us if we decide to fight. When we know there will be a time to fight, this awareness allows us to brace for impact and to battle it out, until the end. And sometimes, fighting is as simple as feeling fully and suffering willingly.

Like you taught me, never back down from a bully, and pain is the biggest bully in our lives. Sometimes students need to remind the teacher…

The One About Doubt

Mom,

I still have a hard time believing in myself. I think of all the things I want to do, and then I might get motivated, and then that familiar feelings creeps in. Old man doubt comes to hang out and makes sure I reconsider everything. Doubt lets me know the odds are bad and that my goals will never come true. And, by the time he leaves my mind and heart- I reconsider my whole life. He makes sure to let me know I will never actually make it happen. Or if it does happen it's meaningless. He's a constant visitor and I don't like it when he comes around. Life is much better when I'm motivated and feel like I can conquer the world. I would like it if he would stay away forever. I hate doubting myself, but I do. I know better than to believe the doubtful thoughts but I do. It's a constant battle, mom. Maybe doubt serves a purpose, but I don't know what that purpose is. Doubt has been with me ever since I can remember.

$$\bullet\ \bullet\ \bullet$$

Can doubting ourselves serve a purpose? I think so. Doubt is here to see if we are going to make a real decision instead of just hoping on a goal, or only participate when it's easy. The real reason Mr. Doubt comes around is to see if we are going to move forward even as Mr. Doubt talks our ear off. Do our actions match our hopes and dreams. Do the daily decisions we make prove to Mr. Doubt that we are committed to our goals?

It doesn't matter if I have regular conversations with Mr. Doubt, as long as I'm committed and take the action that proves my commitment. When we are truly dedicated doubt doesn't matter. Doubt is normal, but it doesn't determine our response. After a while, something happens. If we continue to take action, Mr. Doubt starts to come by less and less. We hardly hear from him because he knows it doesn't matter what he says. He cannot change our minds because we have proven our decisions time and time again through real action.

This is my internal battle, and it doesn't matter who tries to pump me up or make me believe in myself. Outside validation means nothing to Mr. doubt. I must fight this battle alone.

If our decisions and actions tell the world that we believe it can happen, eventually, we'll believe it ourselves. Life is a constant feedback loop, and this loop can be tricked to work for us instead of against us. At some point, there is no choice but to believe in yourself, because all the evidence says "She's going to do it, no matter what."

The One About the Bully

Mom,

During our talk today you told me that deep in your heart, you want to be clean and sober and I could tell that you absolutely meant it. But I see doubt in your eyes and it makes me sad. I want to take this burden from you but once again I'm helpless. I can't make your pain go away. I see these cycles in your life and it hurts. It hurts to see you fall down again and again. It hurts to see you be ashamed of yourself. There is no shame in having problems-there is only shame when we pretend our problems aren't there. I wish I could help. I wish I could save you. I can't stop your bully and it makes me feel like a failure.

. . .

You have a drug problem, there I said it! There has been one common thread that runs through everything bad in your life. It doesn't make you a bad person- it makes you a normal person. You're normal for having struggles, so don't feel any shame. I fight my struggles daily, so you're not alone at all.

Everyone has a bully trying to push them around, for some its food, sex, money, lying, and every other thing you could imagine. You're normal for having struggles, so don't' feel any shame. You have to fight! This is the bully that has constantly beaten you down, stole your lunch money, made you steal, made you lie, snatched your happiness, and made your self-esteem vanish. It's the bully that has hurt your kids, your friends, family and even innocent strangers. And if being bullied is not bad enough, I've seen you take it out on yourself instead of the bully! You stop believing in yourself and start to believe that this is all you'll ever be, a woman who struggles with addiction. You have to stand up to this bully just like you taught me as a little kid. You always told me "When you find yourself in a fight, fight your ass off until it's finished!" You're in a fight, mom. You're in a fight-fight back!

You will not be by yourself, but you have to do it alone. On your darkest hour, there you are, with yourself. When you look in the mirror and lie-the woman looking back at you knows the truth.

I used to think that you chose drugs over me, but I know that's not true. You were choosing drugs over yourself. Afraid of feelings, refusing to acknowledge that little girl you still haven't healed. You must acknowledge the past if you ever want to look that little girl in her eyes and let her know you love her and that you forgive her. You must recognize your past, guide her in forgiving those that have hurt her. You can be that little girls hero if you're willing.

It's time to feel, and it's time to heal that little girl. It's time to release the woman screaming to come out. The woman that I love so much.

My Last Letter

Mom,

I know this might feel like an intervention where I ask you to change for me. It's not, it's an invitation to be happy. I've prayed and prayed to see you happy and I have never stopped. It has been my biggest desire for as long as I can remember.

Happiness doesn't just happen though, it's an earned reward. It's earned by having hard conversations, keeping promises to yourself, doing what you say you'll do, forgiving those who have hurt you, forgiving yourself, being honest with the person in the mirror and making the choice to face all obstacles head on. Facing the past- and dealing with it no matter the pain involved. These are not easy things to do, but in my experience, they lead to happiness.

It's an invitation to be the woman I remember as my mom. I said I would be honest with you when I started this. So… You weren't always there for me, but when you were you were my biggest fan. You didn't make it to many football games, but when you were there everyone knew it because you cheered so loud and hard. You weren't always there to protect me, but when you were there, you were there long enough to teach me to be tough, resourceful, and to always follow my instinct. You didn't always show your love, but when you did you showed me a love that goes all the way in and tattoos my soul. A love that I can't forget. When you are clean and sober you're one of the best women I have ever been around. That's who I miss, my Mom.

Our relationship has been rocky and full of ups and downs but it has taught me so many important lessons. It's taught me that all people are more alike than different. It's taught me that everyone has their battles that nobody knows they are fighting. It has taught me that darkness makes light brighter, and darkness can not ever put out a shining light. But, there is one lesson that stands above all others. The most important lesson our relationship has taught me is how to love.

My love for you can't be described. There is nothing you could do to make me love you any more than I already do. You might think if you did this or that I would love you more, but the truth is, love isn't at it's best when everything is perfect. Love shows itself the best when things are broken, ugly, messy, complicated, and at their most difficult. When things are at their worst, love is at it's best.

It gets to shine when everything is dark. Love doesn't keep score of mistakes and neither have I.

When I started writing these letters I thought I was writing them for you, but as I went deeper and deeper I realized I was writing them for me. I was writing them for that little boy who never has never forgiven himself for not being able to protect you, to save you. It has been a lifelong struggle to feel good enough and not constantly feel like a failure, but I am letting that little boy go now. I am letting him be a little boy, the little boy of my past. He doesn't need to carry any guilt or shame for not being a man because he is a boy and I've discovered how to love him.

This journey has been, well, unexpected to say the least, but It all makes sense now. I cannot be your hero, but I can help you back up when you fall. I can give you a shoulder to cry on. I can hug you when you feel unhuggable. I can be easy on you when you're too hard on yourself and I can be hard on you when you're being too easy on yourself. I can be your biggest fan and cheer you on. I can be your son.

I will always be your little boy but you have helped me reveal the man. I need to thank you for that because that man, is the man I'm proud to be. That man embraces his past, feels everything deeply, and is constantly striving to meet that next version of himself.

Thank you, thank you for teaching me how to love. There is no other woman I would rather call Mom.

Do you feel that? Love never fails and most importantly, love heals.

Your son,

Mikel

P.S.- I almost forgot to answer your question. I can say without a doubt, your kids are going to be okay and we believe in you.

Dear Reader

My mom in her true colors allowed me to put these letters into a book because it might help someone, somewhere. Please tell one person about these letters.

If you want to see some of my favorite pictures of Mom and receive a notice when my next book is out, please click the link below.

Click here to see favorite moments with Mom

Follow me:

- ➢ @bookssavedmyass on Instagram
- ➢ Mikel.billstrom@gmail.com if you would to email me

9 781793 924506